Contemplative Growth and Development

Dr.FrankLayman

First published by Lowe Publishing November 2016
lowepublishing2@gmail.com

Lowe Publishing acknowledges credit to: use of free domain
images by Claude Monet, Edouard Manet, Mary Cassatt and
Paul Cezzane which fall under public domain.

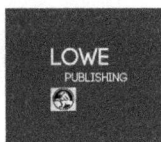

LOWE
PUBLISHING

ISBN 978-0-9979213-2-8

Published and Printed in the United States of America

Thank you
to all who have supported me,
read my work,
and strived to apply the
approaches and lessons to
improve and grow.

I am dedicating this work to you
and committing myself more
to help all those who want to make a
positive change.

"A good Person out of the treasure
of their heart
brings forth that which is good. "
Luke

BOOKS BY: DR.FRANKLAYMAN

SUCCESS THROUGH LOGICAL THINKING #1

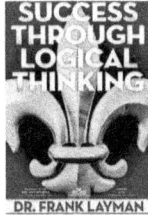

REFLECTIONS TO SUCCESS #2

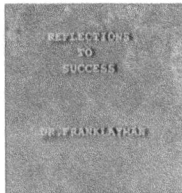

Daily Reflective Growth #3

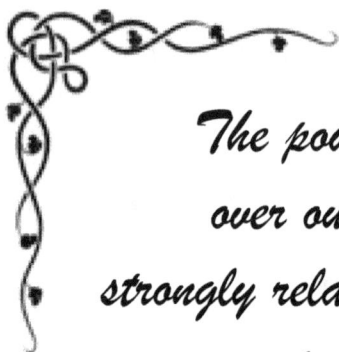

The power we have over our thoughts strongly relates to the power we exert over our lives.
Dr. FrankLayman

If you want to grow as a person you have to travel outside your comfort zone.
Dr. FrankLayman

The tributaries of wellness are the quality of our thoughts and behavior. Dr. FrankLayman

Power is a force and force requires effort.
Focused effort is far more powerful. So as you develop yourself,
you propel forward away from the you, you once where and closer to the higher order self.

That said we never abandon or reject our inner self only work in earnest to improve upon it.
Dr.FrankLayman

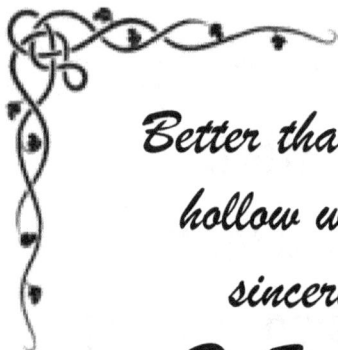

Better than a thousand
hollow words, is one
sincere action.
Dr. FrankLayman

No one can flourish and be happy
without making a conscious effort to
achieve and a choice to revel.
Dr. FrankLayman

Rather than a portraying of self,
just be yourself.
Dr. FrankLayman

Think, be and behave
in a
positive and helpful manner.

Don't intend to do
but instead
do and do in earnest and
being true to yourself.
Find the importance that
sincerity of mind has
when aligned with action
by engaging in it.
Dr.FrankLayman

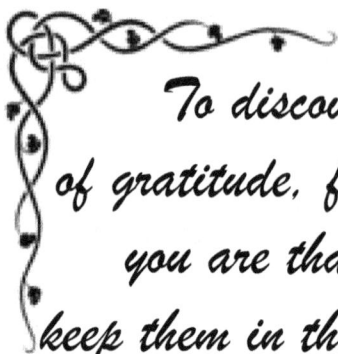

To discover the peace
of gratitude, find all the things
you are thankful for and
keep them in the forefront of your
mind. Dr. FrankLayman

To expand your universe, you must
expand your mind.
Dr. FrankLayman

To find the destination you seek
follow the path on the pages created
by those who have already forged a
way. Dr. FrankLayman

Consider for a moment where peace is found.
It is found in the stillness of a strong mind.
A mind trained to be quiet of neural chatter, self doubt, and regret.
Peace is a choice
we have to decide on it.
It is a goal, an objective and we have to know how to pursue it.
Peace doesn't find you, you find it.
Dr.FrankLayman

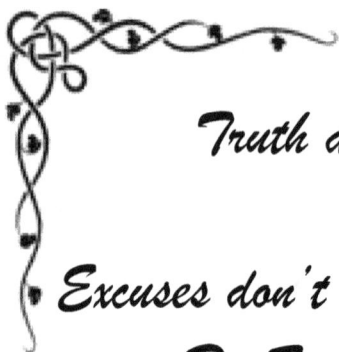

Truth and Ethics

Excuses don't conceal the truth.
Dr. FrankLayman

It is in action where true intent is
revealed.
Dr. FrankLayman

Let no one leave your presence not
better for the encounter.
Dr. FrankLayman

Truth is so powerful yet we often want to conceal it.

It is easier in the short term to tell a lie than to face the truth.

Truth is a virtue that in itself yields reward.

It should be translated in terms of action as transparency.

True and transparent thoughts yield to true and transparent actions. Those are the ones that impact others and humanity in a very positive way.

Dr.FrankLayman

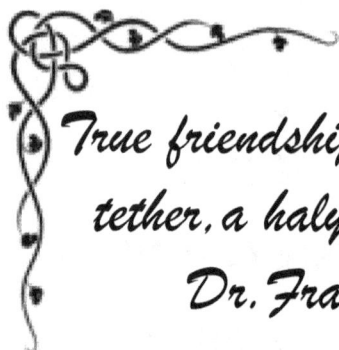

True friendship is a life line, a tether, a halyard, an anchor.
Dr. FrankLayman

We are not defined merely by what we do, but what we constrain ourselves from doing.
Dr. FrankLayman

Who Tries Triumphs!
Dr. FrankLayman

There is something
so pure in truth,
be it the truth of friendship,
action, or courage.
Most will wilt at its calling
ever knowing how glorious
the vulnerability of it is.
That once you have
developed yourself,
the fear of the vulnerability
no longer exists and that all that
comes from it is joy.
Dr.FrankLayman

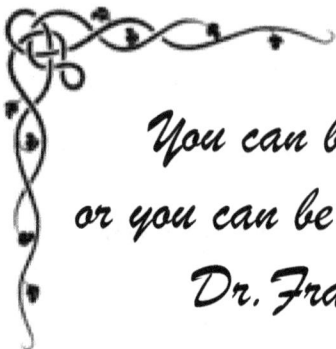

*You can be idle hoping
or you can be active achieving.*
Dr. FrankLayman

*Your will to persevere and overcome
will determine your ultimate
triumphs and destination.*
Dr. FrankLayman

*You can't advance from a defensive
posture.*
Dr. FrankLayman

The most profound gift we are given
is that we can act in selflessness.
To just act detached from thought is
careless at the least and reckless
to self and others.
We would not want to squander a gift,
yet, everyday we are faced with the
option to do or do not, to act for good
or not, to build or destroy,
to quit or persevere.

Think, be, behave and act in the
positive never wilting or relenting and
you will achieve the inverse of regret.
Dr.FrankLayman

Love and Kindness

*A mind at peace centering its
force on Goodness, Kindness,
and Love has no match.
Dr. FrankLayman*

*Just because you aren't accepted by
everyone, doesn't mean you aren't
accepted by those who matter most.
Dr. FrankLayman*

*No matter where you are or what you do
you have the capability to touch people
and impact the world.
Dr. FrankLayman*

Love and kindness
are the most
enduring and impactful
of forces.
They will endure long after hate fails.

They are a choice
and all choices begin
in the recesses of our mind.
Once we choose them
within the choice itself
resides peace and wisdom.

Dr.FrankLayman

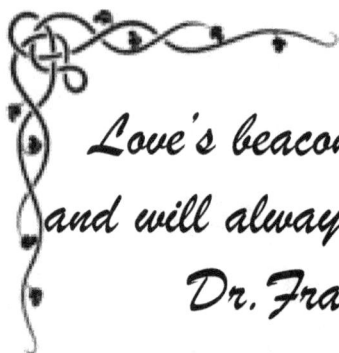

*Love's beacon will never dim
and will always guide you home.*
Dr. FrankLayman

*The noble purpose of wanting to
love more then want of being loved
leads to a selfless mission to
serve + a selfish mission to achieve
happiness*
Dr. FrankLayman

*The Sun shines brightest above the
clouds.*
Dr. FrankLayman

I found my life
when I realized my capacity
to love and serve.
To demonstrate love in a
meaningful way, we must take
skilled actions that help others.
A selfless mission
noble in intent, purpose and results
provided with the brightness of joy.
Love peace and joy
are what we are all seeking.
Imagine if it was what we all would be
willing to strive to give.

Dr.FrankLayman

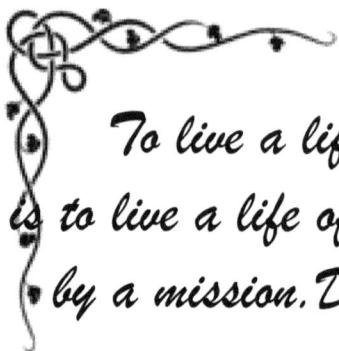

To live a life of happiness
is to live a life of love that is driven
by a mission. Dr. FrankLayman

Wear your scars on the outside as
badges of courage and resilience.
Never let them permeate to the
inside where they can diminish your
heart and its capacity to love and
hope. Dr. FrankLayman

To have Happiness you must define
it, seek it, express it, and share it.
Dr. FrankLayman

I want you to be strong enough and brave enough to never let anyone diminish your capacity to love and be loved.

Not to fear loss, failure, or rejection but to grow strong in them. Don't let another's words or actions, no matter how violent ever discourage you from a future attempt to love.

Do not let anyone diminish the inner you. Fight and work for peace, balance, and love in your mind and the actions manifested from its thoughts will resonate.

Dr.FrankLayman

Wisdom, Understanding & Peace

In the pursuit of greater knowledge there is always opportunity. Dr. FrankLayman

A positive change in our thinking is going to move our lives in a positive direction. Dr. FrankLayman

No matter how hard you are hit never let anyone knock the optimism out of you. Dr. FrankLayman

The core of who we are unrefined, sheltered, or undeveloped would not be.

The high order achievements of wisdom and peace have to be sought and many times they are attained not in the calm, but in the storm.

It is the crucible of learning but once attained it can be taken with us to solve new problems or be creative in our attempts and efforts to better ourself and world around us.

Dr.FrankLayman

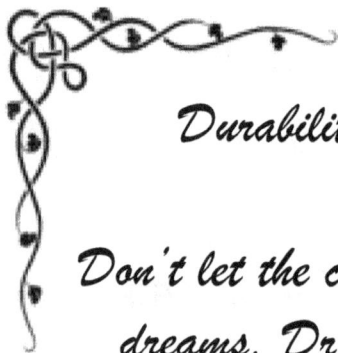

Durability & Legacy

Don't let the critics dictate your dreams. *Dr. FrankLayman*

Failure is a strong lens under which we can see clearer to a more successful future outcome. *Dr. FrankLayman*

I am working on a life though sometimes it seems unreachable. I am working on a life of purpose and hope. I am working on a life not waiting for it and I know it will arrive. *Dr. FrankLayman*

Insincerity adds very little to advancement, so discern it and the people who it comes from.
Base your assessment of self, on yourself and those who are honest and sincere. Be an active participant in the decisions that form your future.

Ensure the counsel you seek is honest true and without ulterior motives. Should you fail and we will, don't label it failure but in-depth understanding and future insights.
Commit to your own greater self by committing to it and working at it.

Dr.FrankLayman

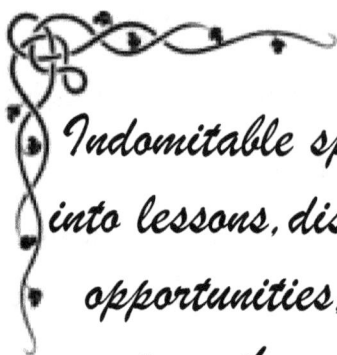

Indomitable spirit makes trials into lessons, disappointments into opportunities, weaknesses into strengths, and failures into successes. Dr. FrankLayman

Our legacy is not built on hope alone but is created by action. Dr. FrankLayman

Plan and Work for the future, learn from the past, but live in the now. Dr. FrankLayman

We tend to under value the
importance and effectiveness
a positive mindset has on us.

It can be transforming
yet we must balance it with
reason, dedication, strategy,
planning and execution to build
our great body of work.

We call it life and what follows is
- Our Legacy
Dr.FrankLayman

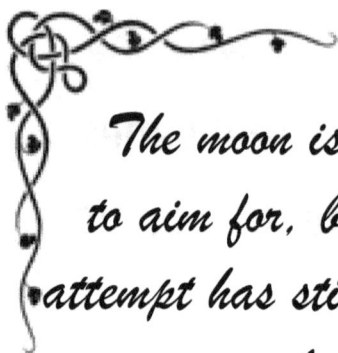

The moon is a great target to aim for, but if missed the attempt has still resulted in your launch.

Dr. FrankLayman

The Possibilities are countless when we are embolden to act.

Dr. FrankLayman

The real quest for success is found within.

Dr. FrankLayman

Don't search for success
as it is not a destination, it is the
progressive development of self.

It is not the same for all, we have no
standard to measure it, except
whether or not it gets us closer to
happiness, peace and self fulfillment.

That is significant enough to
last the test of time and can be
carried then passed forward.

Dr.FrankLayman

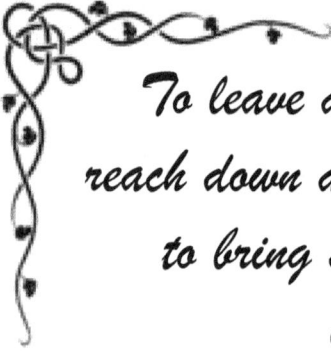

To leave a legacy is to reach down and lend a hand to bring someone else up.
Dr. FrankLayman

You advance through the triumph of trying.
Dr. FrankLayman

We are who we develop ourselves to be.
Dr. FrankLayman

If you find yourself on the wrong
trajectory, it is not too late
to make a few simple changes that will
allow a new path.

You must have the will not just the want to
improve. It also helps to have an effective
approach.
Most will grow weary of trying, fatigue
from failure - don't.

Don't fall into that trap of surrender.
Rebel against that mindset and transform
your thoughts and actions by starting in
the now.

Dr.FrankLayman

Wisdom -
Application of knowledge, logic,
sound judgement + experience
to allow consistent, effectiveness,
positive thoughts + behaviors.
Dr. FrankLayman

Wisdom gained is peace restored.
Dr. FrankLayman

Wisdom Grants a wealth of
success.
Dr. FrankLayman

The ultimate progression of
self-development isn't just for material
success, it is far more than that.
It was known in older cultures and
respected, but the pursuit and willful
obtainment of wisdom and all that
accompanies it.

To find wisdom we must develop ourselves
in the pillars and be anchored in the
cornerstones.
To find wisdom we must seek truth and
understanding in our thoughts, actions
and experiences.

Dr.FrankLayman

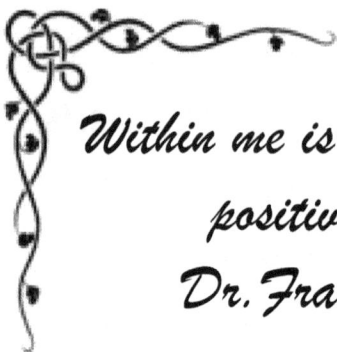

Within me is the catalyst for positive change.
Dr. FrankLayman

Work your plan until your plan works.
Dr. FrankLayman

You're not who you were which allows you to be something more.
Dr. FrankLayman

Seek to grow in what is of value
and worthy of focusing on.
Think on those things worth thinking
upon.

Act on what is noble of action in a way
that provides the greatest good and
positive impact.
There are six virtues seek them in your
thoughts and align them with your words,
reactions, behaviors and actions.

The six virtues are
temperance, wisdom, courage, humanity,
justice, and transcendence.
Dr.FrankLayman

Emotional

Courage is what causes us to push through the comfort of being dormant.
Dr. FrankLayman

Courage is a calculated risk worth taking.
Dr. FrankLayman

Courage Counts!
Dr. FrankLayman

I often reflect upon the triumph of trying and what goes into it.

The decision, character, determination, and self efficacy it takes to make the choice to try.

Summon up your courage don't shrink in times of difficulty or opportunity, but rise. Rise in your faith, belief, skills and courage to take that step forward.

To take that calculated risk and move forward to the unexplored ground and find yourself by not fearing failure.

Dr.FrankLayman

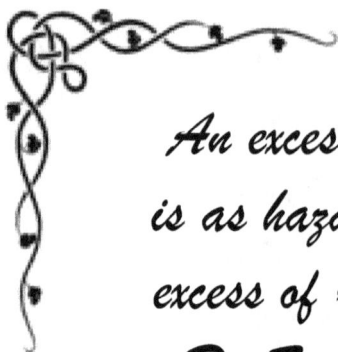

*An excess of caution
is as hazardous as an
excess of recklessness.
Dr. FrankLayman*

*Do not limit the potential heights of
tomorrow with the weight of
yesterday.
Dr. FrankLayman*

*Frustration is looking past this
moment you have to a future moment
you want. Dr. FrankLayman*

To navigate the landmines of life's journey, we need to be balanced in our thinking.

Don't let the past failures, hardships or negative experiences bind you and your thoughts. They can act as an anchor holding us in one place.

We can't reach our destination anchored in one place. Be free of them and let your mind soar to higher heights.
Dr.FrankLayman

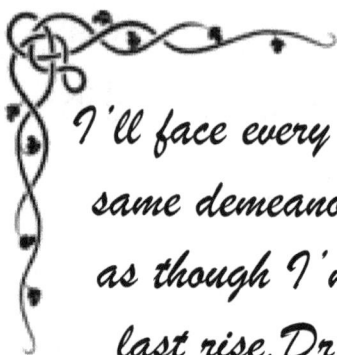

I'll face every adversity with the same demeanor as every favor, as though I'm racing over the last rise. Dr. FrankLayman

Let your mind go of the things weighing you down and allow it to gather to it all the things that will elevate you. Dr. FrankLayman

No matter the circumstance, if you have taken time to develop yourself, you can combat the negative and impress on the situation your positive. Dr. FrankLayman

We press into every situation we are in.
What impression do you want to make?
Start from the end and work backward.

I want to press into life with enthusiasm
and effectiveness, with a willingness to be
helpful to others and humanity.
How could I do that if I don't choose the
thoughts that will result in the actions I
have chosen?
Those things must align - thoughts,
intentions, effort, skill and action to gain
our objective. The quality of choice comes
from the quality of training and refinement
we put ourself through.

Dr.FrankLayman

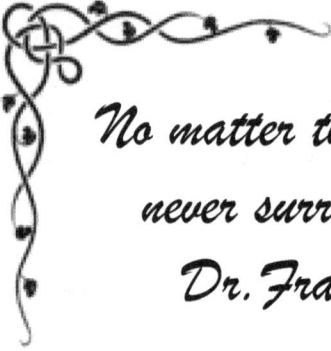

No matter the circumstance never surrender trying.
Dr. FrankLayman

Pain is the greatest bully and its antidote is hope and hard work.
Dr. FrankLayman

Rebel against stagnation in your work, relationships, mind and body – RAGE!
Dr. FrankLayman

Water that remains stagnant becomes toxic. Fear and pain causes resistance
to do and therefore to be and act. There is an untapped well within us that can move us, elevating us over the fear. But it is within us to tap into it to demand better than acceptance.

It takes work and deliberate thoughtful intent and determination to draw out these attributes and possess them, creating, and form them into a better world and future.
Dr.FrankLayman

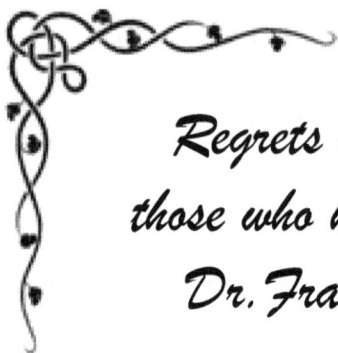

Regrets are only for those who have given in.
Dr. FrankLayman

Achievement has a rippling effect that penetrates all aspects of our life.
Dr. FrankLayman

I want you to strike as a hammer with the intent of shattering the chains of indifference and acceptance when it comes to building your destiny. Dr. FrankLayman

Great things
come from
small deliberate steps
made each day.

The success of today came
from the efforts of
our past, as the
success of tomorrow
shall come from
our effort in today.

Dr.FrankLayman

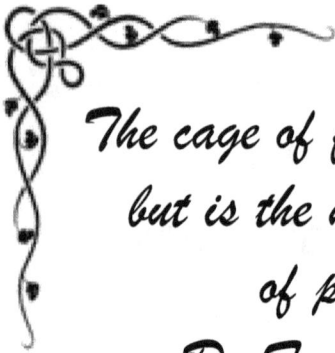

The cage of fear has no bars
but is the most confining
of prisons.
Dr. FrankLayman

The conquest of the mind is the
conquest of success.
Dr. FrankLayman

The only limits on life are those our
fear imposes.
Dr. FrankLayman

Fear is a protective mechanism
but it can also be a bully.

One that suppresses our dreams
and limits our potential.

It is a heavy chain that if worn
over time will
oppress,
bind,
and enslave.
Dr.FrankLayman

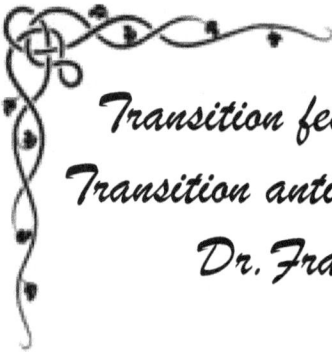

Transition feared is abysmal.
Transition anticipated is infinite.
Dr. FrankLayman

Summon up your mental toughness and press on. Don't waver in your resolve until you are satisfied in your journey.
Dr. FrankLayman

We need to learn how to motivate ourselves when our irrational mind attempts to convince us there is no hope in trying. Dr. FrankLayman

Throughout life there are many times we will be challenged by change.
We will be challenged by doubt of the future, doubt in ourselves, and doubt by the barriers that are always present.

We will have to summon up our courage and press on and we will have to choose wilt or will.

The reservoir of courage is within us and it also has to be trained. Don't underestimate or overlook it.

Dr. FrankLayman

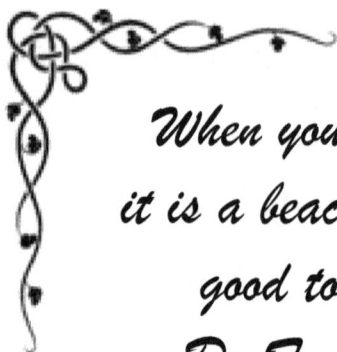

*When you are positive
it is a beacon that allows
good to find you.*
Dr. FrankLayman

*While there are a lot of tools
for success, the greatest are
logical thinking and rational
behavior. Dr. FrankLayman*

*Your life well lived
is your reward.*
Dr. FrankLayman

Proof of life comes from
a progressive life
and a legacy worth leaving.

That doesn't just happen,
you have to design it,
live it,
and embrace it.

Allow it to grow and build
to a crescendo.
Dr.FrankLayman

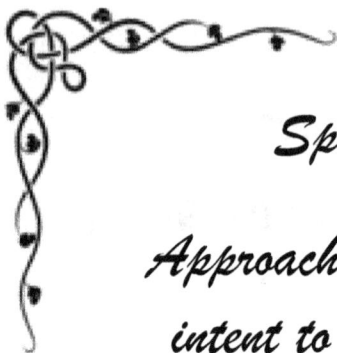

Spiritual

Approach life with the
intent to improve it.
Dr. FrankLayman

Be about your dreams!
Dr. FrankLayman

Embrace the struggle, love it,
know it as a friend who works to
get you better and stronger.
Dr. FrankLayman

Intent is pivotal to outcome.
Stay alert to your inner self and don't suppress your dreams because they are hard.
Don't stop working on them because they seem to far.
Don't relent because the barriers are too high.
Know at the outset you will be challenged.
Set your mind to smile in the face of adversity with the understanding that resistance builds strength.
Dr.FrankLayman

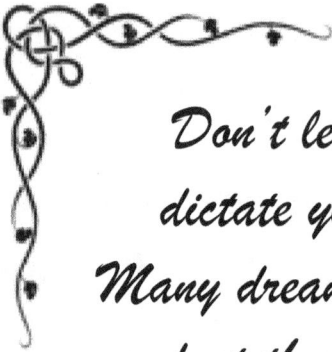

*Don't let the critics
dictate your dreams.
Many dreams are symbolic
and at the same time real
because reality is shaped by
belief and perception.
Dr. FrankLayman*

*Happy are they that don't stand
idly by but fight to see their dreams
realized. Dr. FrankLayman*

*It isn't work if it brings us closer
to your true self. Dr. FrankLayman*

When your dreams and your vocation are in opposition,
you will struggle to find peace.
When you align your dreams, mission and vocation,
peace and happiness will prevail.
During the journey to your dreams, you will encounter barriers,
one of many is the hack, the critic, those who neither create, help or grow.
They just like to provoke, deter, and or create doubt.
Steele yourself up, align your dreams, work and mission.
Interlace your life and your vocation and free yourself of the burden.
Dr.FrankLayman

May your today
be the best thing
that happened to your tomorrow.
Dr. FrankLayman

No matter what you are facing,
Be always Encouraged and
Be always Hopeful.
Dr. FrankLayman

Peace is reached by being active in
what brings you joy, holds purpose
and develops you.
Dr. FrankLayman

We search for happiness in the wrong places.
There is no formula for it and each of us will have to decide how we will achieve it.
As for me, I choose Peace!
I will let it cascade over me and fill me up.
I will immerse myself in it and then carry it with me as I move through life.
Dr.FrankLayman

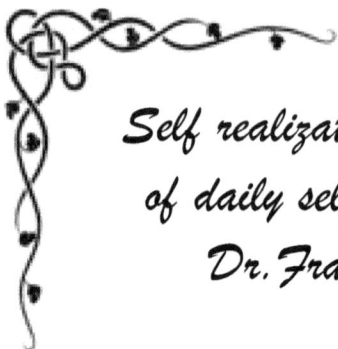

Self realization is the result
of daily self development.
Dr. FrankLayman

Spend a day being grateful, kind,
loving, encouraging, patient,
thoughtful, sincere, selfless and you will
see how transformational and powerful
life can be.
Dr. FrankLayman

The gifts you possess were never meant
for your personal gain alone, but to be
bestowed upon the world freely and
graciously given to humanity.
Dr. FrankLayman

We all get hurt, have fears and suppress our inner self at times and/or overtime.

What we do to emerge rather than hide will dictate our course.

All of us have the choice for a better tomorrow by embracing positive thinking, being happy, grateful and strategic about the map we navigate our path with.

Dr.FrankLayman

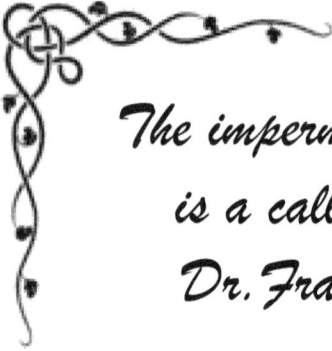

The impermanency of life
is a call to Action.
Dr. FrankLayman

The intent of being in harbor is not
to hide from the storm,
but to prepare for the journey.
Dr. FrankLayman

You want to prevail indefinitely,
shine a light so bright nothing or
no one can ever extinguish it.
Dr. FrankLayman

Enjoy life and make it happy.

Choose and find joy in it all.
It is fragile and finite.

Don't squander it, waste it
or let it slip away.

Embrace it, enjoy it, lighten it
for you and others.

Dr.FrankLayman

*Social-seeking or enjoying
the companionship of others.*

*A Great person like a great river
does not refuse even the
smallest contributory.
Dr. FrankLayman*

*If you want to grow as a person
you have to travel outside your
comfort zone. Dr. FrankLayman*

*Let's not merely say that we love each
other; let us show the truth.
Dr. FrankLayman*

A person of true development,
one who has arrived at
wisdom and peace,
understands the value of
experience,

sees all the good in others and

is willing to sacrifice effort and
time
to guide others to the
radiant glow of enlightenment.
Dr.FrankLayman

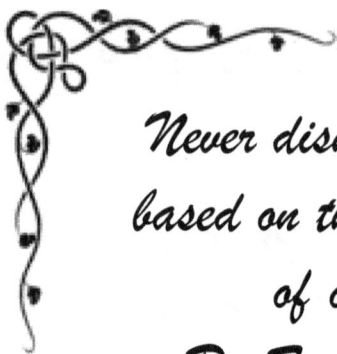

*Never dismiss yourself
based on the judgements
of others.*
Dr. FrankLayman

*People won't value your strength
until they trust your heart.*
Dr. FrankLayman

*Rather than a portraying of self,
just be yourself.*
Dr. FrankLayman

Sincerity is a key dimension to an authentic life.

Live in honesty to yourself and the world.

Never hide who you are from yourself or others.

If there are those around you who cannot accept your authentic self, remove yourself from them.

Don't allow others the privilege of you, who don't deserve you.

Plant your positive in ground worthy of receiving it.

Don't impose negativity on others and create a barrier to it.

Be strong in who you are and work to be worthy of that confidence.

Dr.FrankLayman

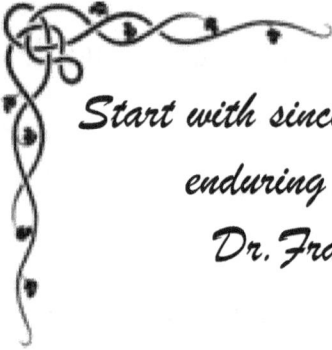

Start with sincerity to end with an
enduring relationship.
Dr. FrankLayman

Stay and be in this moment, enjoying it
for its challenge or pleasure
and yield to it your best.
Dr. FrankLayman

You beat negative circumstances with
Positive Thoughts and Actions.
Dr. FrankLayman

We will all have our hardships,
trials and disappointments to face.
Face them with a strong mindset
on positive thoughts and deliberate
strategic positive actions that are
mindful.
Once you still your mind and steel
yourself up and grow brave by the
experiences of life, share that insight
and strength.
Let it better you and infuse it into
your relationships.

Dr.FrankLayman

Leadership

Every great act is preceded by a positive thought and strong motivation.

Dr. FrankLayman

I am awakening to a new chapter of my life, one that opens up new pages of opportunities to help others and advance myself.

Dr. FrankLayman

I am interested in helping others by applying my approach of daily self development, to achieve a higher state of understanding and performance that allows growth and success, from the positive power that resides within.

Dr. FrankLayman

66

There is a peace that comes from the satisfaction of hard work. That is executed in a way that gets positive outcomes and results and that impact our lives and the world around us.

The greater we train for those moments, the more effective we are in achieving them.

Happiness and peace are found in success.

I define success as the progressive development of self.

Growth is evidence we are not neglecting the gift of life, that we are striving to press into life and make an indelible mark that will leave a legacy.

Dr.FrankLayman

I want to be a
catalyst of inspiration
(stimulation or arousal of the mind,
feelings, to special or unusual activity or
creativity) to think more logically then
provide motivation (desire to do; interest or
drive) to sustain the change that
ultimately leads to achievement.
Dr. FrankLayman

In business respect is demonstrated by
responsiveness and actions.
Dr. FrankLayman

Leadership is an action not a position.
Dr. FrankLayman

We can't avoid the
changes and transitions
we face in
our tomorrow.

We have to prepare for them now
and stay invested
in ourself
never neglecting who we are
and what we can become.

Dr.FrankLayman

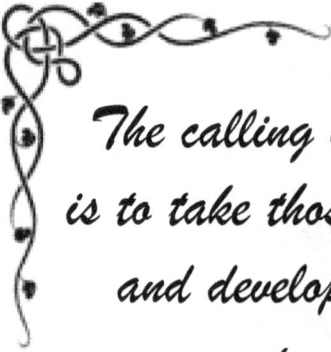

*The calling of a true leader
is to take those in their charge
and develop them to their
greatest potential.*
Dr. FrankLayman

*The currency of success is positive
thinking, thoughtful planning,
strategic execution, rational behavior
and progressive performance.*
Dr. FrankLayman

The Doer Does!
Dr. FrankLayman

Work hard for what you want and don't relent.

Work on the extrinsic and intrinsic factors .

The progress that is achieved from success and its consistent results encourages you in your pursuit of growth and development.

Wherever you are with the proper mindset, motivation and approach you can realize success.

Dr.FrankLayman

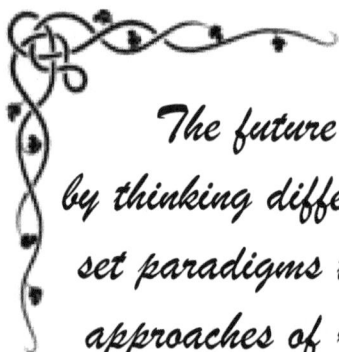

*The future will be forged
by thinking differently and breaking
set paradigms to create innovative
approaches of resolving the tough
challenges before us. Dr. FrankLayman*

*When it comes down to advancing, focus
on approach over condition.
Dr. FrankLayman*

*You can dream, plan, create the greatest
company, but if it isn't managed and
lead to be innovative, fair, and effective, it
won't last.
Dr. FrankLayman*

Many lose their sense of leadership.
They give it away thinking it is too great a responsibility.
It is not a burden, it is an art and anyone can learn to be better at it.
We are all at least a leader of one - ourself.
We can not be complacent with leadership development.
It a critical area of our growth and an imperative to achievement and success.
Don't ignore or neglect your ability to lead embrace it,
form it
and flourish from it.
Dr.FrankLayman

The best leadership development begins with self development.
Dr. FrankLayman

Do the things that will allow the self of tomorrow to realize the victory you had over today.
Dr. FrankLayman

The power we have over our thoughts strongly relates to the power we exert over our lives.
Dr. FrankLayman

There is a desire within all of us to
actualize our potential.
To outgrow our circumstance and
scale higher heights.
Life is a challenging canvas and
we are the art upon it.

Are we going to be satisfied with
what we have created?
We won't be if we don't strive to
develop ourselves,
challenge who we are
and be who we dream.
Dr.FrankLayman

Entrepreneurship

Be always prepared so you will always be present when opportunity knocks. Dr. FrankLayman

Entrepreneur - one who finds a way to get compensated for their passion and happiness.
Dr. FrankLayman

From observation, to thought, to imagination, to reason, to motivation, to action, to results, to refinement is the pathway of success.
Dr. FrankLayman

I will prepare, for my future is awaiting me.
My life is a journey where the beginning, middle and end are seamless
so they flow into each other, but are directed by our care in ourself,
those we love,
and the choices we make,
how we behave,
react and act.

Dr.FrankLayman

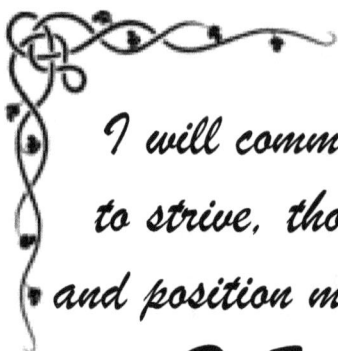

I will commit myself daily
to strive, thoughtfully plan,
and position myself for success.
Dr. FrankLayman

It's never too late to be the success
your've been dreaming about.
Dr. FrankLayman

Rebel against stagnation in your
work, relationships, mind and
body - Rage against Monotony!
Dr. FrankLayman

Life is complex and can
leave us stranded away
from our dreams.
No matter where you are or
what happened,
start now by being aggressive in
choosing the right approach.
One that will change your
trajectory and get you to the
peace and happiness of
something new and worthy
of your effort.
Dr.FrankLayman

Success isn't paved on
a road of excuses.
Dr. FrankLayman

Success is not measured by a value
but by the extent of commitment
to self improvement.
Dr. FrankLayman

Squandered time earns
no future interest.
Dr. FrankLayman

The anonymity of
being a leader,

someone who has the
character
to work selflessly
and expect results

but in a compassionate way,
and starting with ourselves.

Dr.FrankLayman

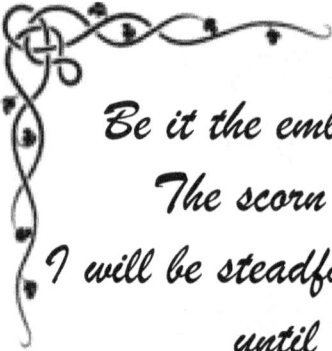

Be it the embrace of the sun,
The scorn of the storm,
I will be steadfast in my continence
until I arrive.
Dr. FrankLayman

Success is a destination. Don't leave
thinking you will arrive without
preparing, planning, and navigating.
Dr. FrankLayman

Success is a journey of a lifetime that
is best when planned but taken day by
day. Dr. FrankLayman

Leadership by its very nature requires
action, effective action requires
critical thinking and courage.
Fear is the most pervasive barrier
to action.
Never let fear be a barrier to your
thoughts and actions.
There are no other means
to affecting positive change
than positive
thoughts and actions.
Dr.FrankLayman

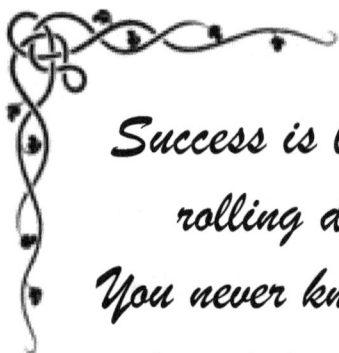

Success is like a snowball
rolling down a hill,
You never know when it can
turn into an avalanche.
Dr. FrankLayman

Success is the progressive
development of self.
Dr. FrankLayman

Success isn't paved on a
road of excuses.
Dr. FrankLayman

The compounding effect is the

gradual building of

efforts laid

end to end that together

result in an

overwhelming outcome.

Dr.FrankLayman

Expertise

*Do something everyday to
improve your station
Dr. FrankLayman*

*Don't allow obstacles to dissuade you
only allow the possibilities
to motivate you.
Dr. FrankLayman*

*Having something to fight for brings
out the best in us. Holding us to the
concentrated effort we need to achieve.
Dr. FrankLayman*

Reaching peace and joy
are often associated
with a selfless mission.
That is an action that leads to worthy
achievement which
improves self worth.
This path isn't an easy one but
it is satisfying, for it brings
with it growth to those who engage
and gifts for those
fortunate enough to be in their
sphere of influence.

Dr.FrankLayman

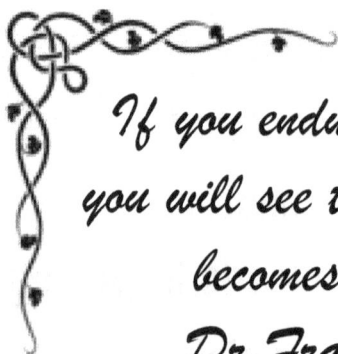

If you endure long enough
you will see that every defeat
becomes a victory.
Dr. FrankLayman

Learn to grow brave in distress—
do not diminish but develop.
Dr. FrankLayman

The arrow unreleased can never
reach its target.
Dr. FrankLayman

There is not only a sense of value
that comes from
the courage to try
but the value of achievement.
There is happiness in achieving,
working hard,
being creative,
and reaching goals
that matter not only to
your journey but to the greater good.
So don't let fear encage you in its
snare, break those chains
and forge forward.
Dr.FrankLayman

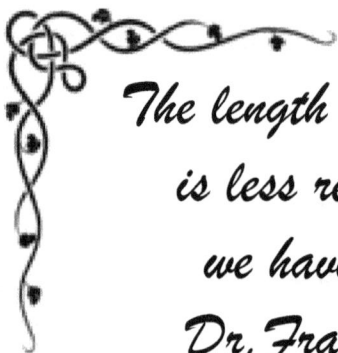

The length of the journey
is less relevant once
we have arrived.
Dr. FrankLayman

When the sails are torn,
break out the oar.
Dr. FrankLayman

When you are at the end of your
road, carve out a path.
Dr. FrankLayman

In the course of the development of our mind, we will not know success without failure.

How we perceive,

internalize,

accept,

react,

learn,

and overcome failure will define us.

It will contribute to the trajectory of our future success.

Will we let it make us bitter or will we allow it to propel us,

fortify us,

and complete us?

Dr.FrankLayman

Health and Wellness

Always be confident
that no matter what, your best future
outcome will prevail.
Dr. FrankLayman

Be aggressive about seeking positive
change by submerging yourself in it.
Dr. FrankLayman

Do the things that will allow the self
of tomorrow to realize the victory you
had over today.
Dr. FrankLayman

It is legacy
not fortune
that changes a life
and thereby
changes humanity.

What legacy will prevail you
and what are you doing now
to ensure it has
an everlasting impact?

Dr.FrankLayman

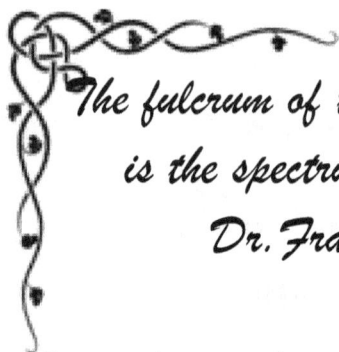

The fulcrum of thinking and feeling
is the spectrum of happiness.
Dr. FrankLayman

I Wish all who are searching for peace
and happiness to realize and assimilate
the importance of actively seeking:
Wholeness, Mindfulness, Harmony,
Completeness, Prosperity,
Judiciousness, Welfare and Tranquility.
Dr. FrankLayman

Improve your physicality with fitness
and you will see a transposition to
mental endurance.
Dr. FrankLayman

94

Create a supportive, motivating and positive internal environment for yourself.

Dedicate yourself to growth and development and allow yourself the opportunity to succeed, be happy and thrive.

It won't be work if you allow yourself to change your mindset and accept a better process by which to evolve.

Dr.FrankLayman

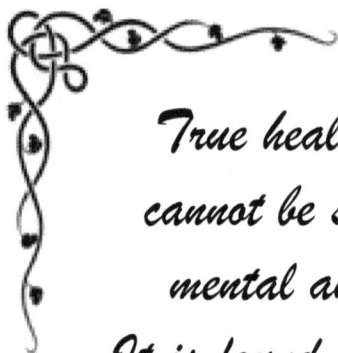

True health & wellness
cannot be separated into
mental and physical.
It is found one part reliant
on the other to be whole.
Dr. FrankLayman

Overcome Barriers by searching for
your strengths + the barrier's
weakness.
Dr. FrankLayman

Let hardship harden your resolve not
your heart.
Dr. FrankLayman

Fortify yourself
with a strong approach to growth
and steel yourself up for
the rough patches ahead
not wilting at the challenge
but rising.
Rising up
after you have been knocked down,
pushed off the page,
or tripped up.
Get up, never,
relent, never stop fighting
for what you know you can
accomplish.
Dr.FrankLayman

MEET THE AUTHOR:DR.FRANKLAYMAN

Dr.Frank's work in self development was sparked by his entrepreneurial ventures and his time in service.

With his mix of self development, enthusiasm, optimism, and self reliance, Dr.FrankLayman emphasizes that we all need to take control of our life.

Advocating that there exists a solution to our hardship, he provides insights for daily growth and development.

American self-help advocate,author, speaker and lecturer.
He advocates: "Approach above circumstance allows for success."

His goal is to help those who want to make a positive change.

Stay connected to stay motivated.

Find me on Twitter.

Look for my websites.

Read the blogs,

Go to my podcasts on Spreaker.com,

Emerging Book:

"The Impact of You"
"Changing Your Destiny By Changing The Conversation You Have With Yourself"

Dr.FrankLayman

www.ingramcontent.com/pod-product-compliance
Lightning Source LLC
LaVergne TN
LVHW041303080426
835510LV00009B/852